LET ME ENCOURAGE YOU

A 30-Day Devotional for Everyday Living

GEORGE ROBINSON

Copyright © 2022 George Robinson.

All rights reserved. No part of this publication may be reproduced, distributed, or transmitted in any form or by any means, including photocopying, recording, or other electronic or mechanical methods, without the prior written permission of the author. Scripture taken from the NEW KING JAMES VERSION®. Copyright© 1982 by Thomas Nelson, Inc. Used by permission. All rights reserved. Scriptures marked TM are taken from the THE MESSAGE: THE BIBLE IN CONTEMPORARY ENGLISH (TM): Scripture taken from THE MESSAGE: THE BIBLE IN CONTEMPORARY ENGLISH, copyright©1993, 1994, 1995, 1996, 2000, 2001, 2002. Used by permission of NavPress Publishing Group.

ISBN: 978-1-943342-10-5 (Paperback)
First printing edition 2022.

LET ME ENCOURAGE YOU
A 30-Day Devotional for Everyday Living

George Robinson
robbierobb06@gmail.com

www.DestinedToPublish.com
Published by Destined To Publish, in the United States of America.

DEDICATION

This book is dedicated to the Father,
the Son, and the Holy Spirit.

ACKNOWLEDGMENTS

I am so thankful for my girls, Deja, Trinity, Sydney, Rhyen, and Neveah, who are my world. My mother, Carolyn Robinson, and brother, Brian Robinson, have always been a great support system to me. I am grateful for my entire family.

I would also like to acknowledge New Jerusalem Church of God in Christ, where under the leadership of the late Bishop Barnett Karl Thoroughgood, I came to know the Lord Jesus Christ.

Finally, at Valley Kingdom Ministries International, under the leadership of Apostle H. Daniel Wilson and Pastor Beverly Wilson, I grew in the Lord, discovered purpose, and began serving in that purpose.

INTRODUCTION

I will never forget August 14, 1999. It was the worst day of my life. I was living in Virginia Beach, Virginia, at the time, while my father, George Robinson Sr. was battling cancer in Calumet City, Illinois, a suburb five to ten minutes south of Chicago. I went home quite often that year to visit him.

I flew in thinking it would be the same routine: I would land, visit him, and then return to Virginia. Upon my arrival at the hospital that day, I exited the elevator only to be greeted by my Uncle Tony, who shared the news that my father had passed. There was a restroom to my right, and I ran into it and broke down. My father, my hero, was gone. Life would never be the same.

At the time of my father's passing, I had begun attending New Jerusalem Church of God in Christ in Virginia Beach, Virginia. However, I wasn't saved. I wasn't ready to give up my sin and totally surrender my life to Christ. My father's passing was a wake-up call that I could no longer gamble with where I would spend my eternity. So in September of 1999, I walked

INTRODUCTION

down the aisle of New Jerusalem Church of God in Christ, where I repented of my sins, believed that Jesus Christ is the Son of God, Who died for my sins and rose again from the dead, and confessed Him as my Lord and Savior.

If I thought my life would never be the same at the passing of my father, I had no idea the journey I was about to embark on after I made that confession that day. I was about to find out just how real Jesus is by way of His Word, a visitation one night, and the reason He placed me on the earth. There is nothing more fulfilling than doing the very things He created you to do.

I didn't grow up in church, so after worship at church that day, I drove to Barnes and Noble and bought my very first Bible. Once I began to read, I couldn't put it down. It is the most fascinating book that I have ever picked up because it is alive. As I read it, it read me. It steered me into the direction of purpose. It was in the Scriptures where 1 Timothy 4:11–16 leaped off the page at me, confirming my assignment from the Lord to teach, preach, and share His Word. At the time of this writing, I've been doing just that for twenty years. The same Bible that has been medicine to me, He has given me the assignment to share so that it can be medicine for others; thus the publishing of this devotional. My sincere prayer is that within the confines of this book will be words that will help you take on each day, over the course of the month.

Before we begin, I have an amazing free offer that you may not have taken advantage of yet. In the beginning Adam and Eve's disobedience to God ushered in death and made us enemies of God. In order for a reconciliation to take place between mankind and God, a sacrifice needed to be made. God's love for us is so great that He sent His Son Jesus (Who agreed) to be that sacrifice

INTRODUCTION

for us. He would die on a cross, and be raised from the dead three days later. This event would enable everyone who puts their faith in Jesus as the Son of God, would also overcome death, and would allow us to no longer be enemies of God. There is also a prepared place for us, where we get to spend an amazing eternity with God. My free offer? Embrace this amazing free gift with no strings attached by saying the prayer below:

> *Lord Jesus, I repent of my sins. I believe that You are the Son of God, Who died for my sins and was raised from the dead. I confess You as my Lord and Savior, and I'm thankful for my new beginning that now begins in You. In Jesus' name. Amen!*

Welcome to the family of God. Find a good Bible-believing church where you can be discipled and grow in your relationship with God.

DAY 1

"Love is patient, love is kind. It does not envy, it does not boast, it is not proud. It does not dishonor others, it is not self-seeking, it is not easily angered, it keeps no record of wrongs. Love does not delight in evil but rejoices with the truth. It always protects, always trusts, always hopes, always perseveres. Love never fails..." (1 Corinthians 13:4–8)

LOVE WINS

If you're reading this, then I'm sure you are aware that the world is infested with evil. You don't even need to leave the house to be made aware of that. Just turn on the news and you'll have all of the proof that you need. However, just because we are surrounded by it doesn't mean we have to become it. While we can't change the whole world, we can make a difference and present something different in our world.

As you go out and face this day, make the commitment right now that love will be your weapon of choice. This means, whoever you encounter, love and everything it entails will be your response. Their impatience will be met with your patience. Their rudeness will be met by your kindness. You will fire off the ammunition of humility and willingness to serve others. You will be God's representative today as His love flows out of you, impacting those who encounter you. As long as you go out armed with this weapon, you can't lose. Why? Because love never fails.

Today's Prayer: Father, I desire to glorify you today. Please enable me to be a living example of your love. In Jesus' name. Amen!

Amen Love Wins

DAY 2

"Yet in all these things we are more than conquerors through Him who loved us. For I am persuaded that neither death nor life, nor angels nor principalities nor powers, nor things present nor things to come, nor height nor depth, nor any other created thing, shall be able to separate us from the love of God which is in Christ Jesus our Lord." (Romans 8:37–39)

MY MIND IS MADE UP

One of the most amazing things about salvation is the peace that Christ can bring to the mind. When the mind is stable, you can be settled, even when everything around you is unstable. When things are falling apart, it is the state of the mind that will determine if you're able to keep it together.

There is nothing more medicinal to the mind in this life than the Word of God, its promises, and understanding who we are in Christ Jesus. So if you're in a poor state of mind, my prayer is that today you will be intentional in drawing nearer to Christ through prayer, praise, worship, and meditating in His Word. Be on the offensive in bombarding your mind with the things of God, so like Paul, you too will be persuaded that "all these things" can't drive a wedge between you and the love of God, which is able to keep you. There are situations and circumstances that are out of our control, but what we can control is being diligent in keeping and protecting the state of our mind. Be healed in your mind and receive the peace that Christ can bring in Jesus' name.

> *Today's Prayer: Father, my mind is made up that You love me. I'm exchanging my anxiety for Your ability to bring peace and comfort to the mind. Thank you, Father for stabilizing my mental state, as I know that I am more than a conqueror. In Jesus' name, Amen!*

I'm exchanging my anxiety for your ability to bring peace and comfort to the mind.

DAY 3

"For God so loved the world that He gave His only begotten Son, that whoever believes in Him should not perish but have everlasting life. For God did not send His Son into the world to condemn the world, but that the world through Him might be saved." (John 3:16–17)

YOU'RE VALUABLE

John Burroughs, who was an essayist in the nineteenth and twentieth centuries, once said, "For anything worth having, one must pay the price…"

For God to be willing to pay the price with the life of His only Son means that you are worth having. You are indeed valuable. It doesn't matter how you were treated by your mother or your father. It doesn't matter who belittled you or abandoned you. It doesn't matter who mishandled you. When it came to you, God didn't go window shopping. He knew exactly who he wanted—you—went into the store, and paid, not with a mastercard but with the Master Himself.

YOU'RE VALUABLE

When we learn to see ourselves through God's eyes, then "men's" evaluation of us through their eyes won't hold any weight. Come out of paralysis because of man's opinion and walk into purpose because of God's provision. Today, hold your head up because you've been chosen to be an heir of God and a joint heir with Jesus Christ. I don't care what they've said, you *are* valuable.

Today's Prayer: Father, I thank you for the reminder of who I am in You. Help me to combat negative words spoken with your words that were spoken concerning me. I now see myself through Your eyes as the apple of Your eye. Thank you for proving my worth to you with the giving of Your Son. In Jesus' name, Amen!

DAY 4

"Therefore, if anyone is in Christ, he is a new creation; old things have passed away; behold, all things have become new." (2 Corinthians 5:17)

A FRESH START

I'm a huge fan of the NBA. If a great player has a bad game, they don't carry that negativity over into the next game. They see the next game as an opportunity for a fresh start. They see the next game as an opportunity to do something new. They understand that the old game, where they may have stunk up the place, is in the past, while the new game is a golden opportunity to do better.

Embracing Christ as the Author and Finisher of our faith provides us the same opportunity to do something new. We may have stunk up the place in our past, but those things are old and have passed away so that we can now embrace the new. Christ doesn't condemn you because of your past, so don't allow others to condemn you either. This is your season to embrace new opportunities. I'm talking about new behavior, new speech, new relationships, and new opportunities to be better, to do better, all made possible by Jesus Christ and with His help.

So shake off the last five years, shake off the last five months, or you may just need to shake off yesterday, because in front of you all things have become new. I heard a pastor say, "The reason why the windshield is so much bigger than the rearview mirror is because where you're going is so much bigger than where you've been." It doesn't matter how you feel today; God has given you the opportunity for a fresh start. Rejoice!

> *Today's Prayer: Father, thank you for not condemning me because of my past. Please help me to forget those things which are behind, reaching forward to those things which are ahead. Father, I embrace and I thank you for the opportunity for a fresh start. In Jesus' name, Amen!*

DAY 5

"Trust in the Lord with all your heart, And lean not on your own understanding; *In all your ways acknowledge Him, And He shall direct your paths."* (Proverbs 3:5–6)

FOLLOW THE YELLOW BRICK ROAD

If you've ever seen the movie *The Wiz* then you know that each character was in search of something. The Scarecrow, the Tin Man, Dorothy, and the Cowardly Lion were all in search of something different, yet they all used the same yellow brick road as the path to get to their destination.

All of us should be in a continual search, not necessarily for what we want, but for what God wants. Though it may differ for each of us, it is beneficial that we all use the same Word of God as our path to get there. Acknowledging the Lord, and His ways, in all that we do should be our "yellow brick road." This will ensure that we get to the destination that God had in mind for us before the foundation of the world. Matthew 6:33 says,

"But seek first the kingdom of God and His righteousness, and all these things shall be added to you."

So when we're in a place of confusion, doubt, or uncertainty, it is seeking the Lord and reading His Word that will allow us to "ease on down" to the place of clarity, hope, and unwavering faith. No matter how far you've veered off course, you are just one decision away from getting on the "yellow brick road," which is the path God intended, thus leading to the destination God intended. It is never too late to "Follow the Yellow Brick Road."

Today's Prayer: Father, I understand that Your path is better than my path. So today I commit to following the "yellow brick road," which will lead me to all that You have for me. In Jesus' name, Amen!

DAY 6

"For whatever things were written before were written for our learning, that we through the patience and comfort of the Scriptures might have hope." (Romans 15:4)

SOMETHING TO LOOK FORWARD TO

Adhering to the suggestion given to him by his significant other, Dana Canedy, First Sergeant Charles Monroe King, wrote letters to his newborn son while overseas. He was killed while in Iraq in 2006. This real-life occurrence was played out in the movie *A Journal for Jordan*, starring Michael B. Jordan. Though his father wouldn't be physically present, the letters, which were "written for his learning" would guide him through the different stages of his life.

We don't have to physically see God to know that He's real. It is His letters written to us by His chosen vessels that can guide us through the different stages of our lives and prove that He's real and that He loves us. The Scriptures were written ahead of time for our learning so that, through all of life's ups and downs, it is the Scriptures that comfort us and bring us hope while in despair. It is the Scriptures that remind us that, while in the valley, we have something to look forward to. Make no mistake about it, your best days aren't behind you; they are in front of you. So look to the hills from whence comes your help; your help comes from the Lord. Whatever challenges you might be facing today as you continue down "the yellow brick road," the Scriptures show you that just up ahead you have "Something to Look Forward To."

Today's Prayer: Father, I admit that my current challenges having clouded my view. Today, I will lie on the comfort of the Scriptures, which will remove the clouds of hopelessness, despair, and fear, allowing me to clearly see that indeed I have something to look forward to. In Jesus' name, Amen!

DAY 7

"And we know that all things work together for good to those who love God, to those who are the called according to His *purpose."* (Romans 8:28)

BECAUSE OF WHAT I KNOW

In Park Forest, Illinois, there is a train that crosses Western Avenue quite frequently. While others are stuck at the train, I've already gotten to the other side of it and continued on to my destination because I know the area. If I didn't know the area, then I would also be stuck at the train. It is because of what I know that I can make it to the other side of this obstacle.

Hosea 4:6 says, *"My people are destroyed for lack of knowledge. Because you have rejected knowledge."* So the question on the table today is not, "What do you see?" The question is, "What do you know?" It is what you know that will enable you to get past what you see.

I see anxiety, but I know that I don't have to be anxious for anything. I know that with prayer and supplication, with thanksgiving, I can make my request known to Him, and His peace, which surpasses all understanding, will comfort and guard my heart and mind in Christ Jesus.

I see depression, but I know that in the presence of the Lord is the fullness of joy and, at His right hand, pleasures forevermore.

I see financial lack, but I know that He is Jehovah Jireh, Who will provide.

Don't let ignorance destroy you. Let the knowledge of His Word revive you, getting you to the other side of that train. Yes, I see the problem, but I also know that it's working together for my good because I love God and I am the called according to His purpose.

> *Today's Prayer: Father, I thank you for the reminder that it is my knowledge of Your Word that will sustain me and keep me moving toward the destination that You have for me. I will not get stuck because of what I see; I will keep moving because of what I know. In Jesus' name, Amen!*

DAY 8

"What then shall we say to these things? If God is for us, who can be against us? He who did not spare His own Son, but delivered Him up for us all, how shall He not with Him also freely give us all things?" (Romans 8:31–32)

HE'S ON MY TEAM

In the documentary *The Last Dance*, which highlights different players from the Chicago Bulls and their team during their championship run in the nineties, a reporter interviewed Steve Kerr regarding the success of the team. Kerr emphasized the importance of having Michael Jordan on the team. Anyone who is a fan of the NBA knows that the success of the Chicago Bulls in the nineties was because of Michael Jordan. It didn't matter what challenges they faced, Jordan ensured they were a team and would get past every one.

I don't know what challenges you are facing, have faced, or will face, but this is a friendly reminder that God is on your team. I heard a pastor say one time, "I have no successful enemies." In other words, if God is on your team, what other team dare come against you and think they'll be victorious? Not only is victory your portion because of God, but with His Son, Jesus, He shall freely give you all things. You already have and will have everything you need to be successful.

So as the fiery darts of depression, anger, betrayal, addiction, lack, and all things sent to paralyze your progression try to hold you back, let God be your go-to person Who has a track record of coming through in the clutch. It doesn't matter what you're facing today, you shall overcome it because God is on your team. Be encouraged!

> *Today's Prayer: Father, I confess that I'm surrounded with issues. I'm also glad that none of these issues are a surprise to You. Thank you, Father, for being on my team, where I know I already have the victory. In Jesus' name, Amen!*

DAY 9

"That's why I don't think there's any comparison between the present hard times and the coming good times." (Romans 8:18 TM)

IT WON'T LAST

I can remember walking into the galley (cafeteria) with my brand new company on my first day of boot camp in the US Navy, and hearing someone who had been there for a while say, "You all might as well give up now."

I believe they were insinuating that not only did we have eight weeks to go, but there were challenges up ahead during those eight weeks. The first five weeks of boot camp, we wore these green belts, also known as "dookie belts." During Weeks Six through Eight, we wore white belts, also known as "sugar belts." When we put on our "sugar belts" in Week Six, it was our indication that our time of obstacles, challenges, and suffering was coming to an end. We were now a long way away from Day One, and we realized that our time in boot camp wouldn't last.

IT WON'T LAST

Life can feel like one big boot camp. We are constantly facing a myriad of obstacles, challenges, and some suffering. But just like my time in boot camp didn't last, these trials that we are going through won't last either. The Scriptures promise that the present sufferings we may be going through aren't even worthy to be compared to the good times ahead. Can I prophesy to you that, whatever trials you've been dealing with, you are now putting on your "sugar belt"? In other words, it's coming to an end, and it won't last. So today, don't lose hope. Please keep the faith, because the truth is that graduation is just up ahead. "It Won't Last."

Today's Prayer: Father, life is filled with so many problems and distractions. Thank you for the reminder of the promise that there are better days ahead. Please help me to stay mindful of these things as I traverse through this boot camp called life. In Jesus' name, Amen!

DAY 10

"The Lord will fight for you, and you shall hold your peace." (Exodus 14:14)

THE LORD'S GOT IT!

In my opinion, Cedar Point is the best amusement park in the country. It has what I like to call "the big boy" roller coasters. While at the top, right before the steep drop, I'll take my hands off the bar that's holding me in and lift them in the air, trusting that the bar holding me in will keep me as I go through the ups and downs, and the twists and turns of the roller coaster. I have successfully made it through every roller coaster I've been on.

It can be hard as individuals to take our hands off situations where we feel we've been wronged, or that seem out of control. We need reminders that, because the Lord is in place, we can lift our hands because the Lord's got it. So today, picture me gently prying your hands off the bars of betrayal, false accusations, worry, anxiety, fear, doubt, and more because the Lord will fight for you so you can rest in that promise. You don't have to respond; the

Lord's got it. You don't have to get revenge; the Lord's got it. You can go to sleep tonight because the Lord's got it. God is no respecter of persons. If He can fend off the Egyptians who were chasing the children of Israel, He can fend off your enemies who are chasing you. There is only one thing for you to do now, and that is lift your hands up, because "The Lord's Got It!"

> *Today's Prayer: Father, I have a tendency to take matters into my own hands. Today, I'm taking my hands off because You fight for me, and I don't want to get in the way of what You have in mind. So I lift my hands, giving You total control. In Jesus' name, Amen!*

DAY 11

"Call to Me, and I will answer you, and show you great and mighty things, which you do not know." (Jeremiah 33:3)

GET READY TO SEE AND HEAR

You probably know by now that life comes with its fair share of problems. You are probably aware that life is full of unanswered questions. You have probably lived in a season where nothing makes sense. You've questioned your purpose, your relationships, your job, and even where you are in life at the moment. Maybe you feel you should be further along than you are. Maybe you are exactly where you want to be, and you're wondering what's next. It is impossible to go through life without questions.

While your family, friends, and associates are maybe great to talk to, and get advice and even some insight from, the ultimate go-to person must be God. There is no one who can answer us and show us His creation, what we need to know and see, like the Creator. He gives us an invitation to call on Him, where He promises to answer. He also promises to show us things we don't know. How rude of us to not accept this invitation with excitement. It's a setup to get closer to God, and I don't mind this setup one bit.

Today is a great day to put the phone down, lift your hands up, and call on God. He can insert light into darkness. He can insert clarity into confusion. He can insert peace into worry. You may no longer be in first grade, but God desires to "show and tell." This is an offer that we can't refuse. As you seek the face of God, get ready with expectation to see and hear.

Today's Prayer: Father, I'm going to stand on Your Word today. I'm going to call on You because I need answers, and I'm looking forward to hearing what you have to say to me and seeing what you desire to show me. Thank you in advance for your plan to reveal. In Jesus' name, Amen!

DAY 12

"For I know the thoughts that I think toward you, says the Lord, thoughts of peace and not of evil, to give you a future and a hope." (Jeremiah 29:11)

THE BIG PICTURE

The children of Israel had been taken captive from Jerusalem to Babylon. While they were in captivity, the Lord sent Word to them from the prophet Jeremiah regarding their future. He talked about a time when they would not be in their current situation because he had plans for them. He had a bright future for them, and even though their present looked bleak, what was waiting for them in their tomorrow looked very promising.

This doesn't surprise me, because even though the children of Israel put themselves in that place, He is a good and merciful God, Who hasn't forgotten them.

Be reminded today that God hasn't forgotten you. Even though your present may look bleak, like the children of Israel in our verse today, God also has plans for you. In other words, what

THE BIG PICTURE

you're currently looking at isn't it. As the saying goes, "Trouble won't last always." Why? It's because of the big picture. Your current picture isn't the final picture. God has bigger things in mind concerning you. Be faithful in this place. Be prayerful in this place. Be led by the Spirit of God in this place. You may feel captive now, but your freedom is on the horizon. What you're looking at isn't the only picture; there is a bigger picture. God has great plans for you.

Today's Prayer: Father, I thank you that You love me, and that You haven't forgotten about me. I'm asking for Your peace as I travel through this current process. I know that You're with me and have great plans for me. I trust You Father through this, and I thank you in advance for the big picture that I have yet to walk into. In Jesus' name, Amen!

DAY 13

"In everything give thanks; for this is the will of God in Christ Jesus for you." (1 Thessalonians 5:18)

THANK YOU!

Whenever we're on the receiving end of anything bad, it is having a heart of gratitude that will help. I don't say it will change the situation, but a heart of gratitude certainly helps. When we look at it as an opportunity to see God show up in our lives in a new way, it can change our perspective. We can see things from an aerial view, instead of at ground level. Every trial is a new opportunity to stand on the promises of God in His Word, and to wait and watch with expectation as He performs His Word. It's another opportunity to experience a side of God that we haven't seen, further proving that He is Who He says He is, and how much He is concerned with and involved in the affairs of our lives. We get to experience His immanence.

So with this in mind, fix your lips to tell Him, "Thank You." You may not understand what's going on, but you can tell Him, "Thank You," that you'll get to see Him reveal. You may not understand how this is going to end, but you can tell Him, "Thank You," that He's in control. You may not like the length of time covering this ordeal, but you can tell Him, "Thank You," for the patience that's being developed. In other words, *"In everything give thanks; for this is the will of God in Christ Jesus for you."* (Thessalonians 5:18) because *"If God be for you, then who can be against you?"* (Romans 8:31). You are going to come out stronger, wiser, and better, but as you travel every step along the way, don't forget to tell God, "Thank You!"

Today's Prayer: Father, I thank you for Your will for my life. I may not understand the process, but because I trust You, I'm going to say thank you that this is all going to come together for my good. I understand that a heart of gratitude can help me physically, mentally, and emotionally, so today I give You praise, and I give You thanks. In Jesus' name, Amen!

DAY 14

"Be anxious for nothing, but in everything by prayer and supplication, with thanksgiving, let your requests be made known to God; and the peace of God, which surpasses all understanding, will guard your hearts and minds through Christ Jesus." (Philippians 4:6–7)

WORRY NOT!

Because we live in a fallen world, life is full of uncertainty. There are plenty of times where we don't know what to say, do, or how to handle any given dilemma. There are things that may need to happen, but we don't know how they're even possible. There are also things that we encounter that will cause us to ask the question, "Why?" When we're staring down the barrel of all of these uncertainties, we can become overwhelmed, stressed, anxious, and worried. This happens when we insist on holding this weight in our hands, instead of placing it all in His hands. One thing I know for sure, and that is that Jesus is a gentleman, and He would love to carry that weight for you.

When the King of kings is in our corner, we don't have to worry about the how, we just need to trust in the Who. Because He is omniscient, or all-knowing, not only is the dilemma not a surprise to Him, but the escape route is already in place. It's not a matter of if it'll work out; it's just a matter of when. Our responsibility in the meantime? We must keep walking by faith and not by sight. We must also be open to the fact that it may not work out how we thought it would, or things may not happen the way we wanted them to, but trust that no matter the outcome, like the sitcom in the fifties, that *"Father Knows Best."* So what do we say to all of these things? Worry not! Allow Him to carry the weight. Get some sleep tonight, resting in the assurance of His presence, power, and provision. Everything is going to be fine. Again, I say, "Worry Not!"

> *Today's Prayer: Father, I'm so grateful that You're a perfect gentleman. Please forgive me for carrying this weight all of this time. Today, I'm making the decision to release it all to You. I trust that You are with me, and have already made a way for me, so I will take heed, and worry not. In Jesus' name, Amen!*

DAY 15

"For we know Him who said, 'Vengeance is Mine, I will repay,' says the Lord. And again, 'The Lord will judge His people.'" (Hebrews 10:30)

LET IT GO

Because we live in a fallen world, we are susceptible to the flaws and evil of man. At some point in your life you have more than likely been done wrong by someone. Someone has betrayed you, lied to you, taken advantage of you, abused you, abandoned you, manipulated you, and of course I could go on. The fact is, because we live in a fallen world, being on the receiving end of these things is inevitable. However, it is our response that can be the difference maker. Your response can either make things better or make things worse. It takes a tremendous amount of discipline and self-control (a fruit of the Spirit) to not allow what we feel like doing in retaliation to override what the Word says do in simply allowing God to take it from here.

LET IT GO

I want to encourage you today that you don't have to get revenge. That is too much responsibility for you, and it gets in the way of what God has in mind. It is pretty safe to say that God's vengeance would be better than your vengeance. So whatever the injustice you have faced, He is the God of justice and the best thing you can do is to take your hands off the entire situation and let it go. God will replenish and restore. Also, the suspects will eventually have to see Him. Get out of the way. Let God do His thing. He knows what He's doing, so the best thing for you to do is to "Let It Go."

Today's Prayer: Father, I admit that it can be hard waiting on Your timing for justice to be served. However, today I relinquish it all to You. Thank you for the reminder that vengeance belongs to You, so I'm letting it go. In Jesus' name, Amen!

DAY 16

"Greater love has no one than this, than to lay down one's life for his friends. You are My friends if you do whatever I command you. No longer do I call you servants, for a servant does not know what his master is doing; but I have called you friends, for all things that I heard from My Father I have made known to you." (John 15:13–15)

A FRIEND OF THE FAMILY

If you've ever watched *Good Times* then you know it was a family of five. You had James, Florida, JJ, Thelma, and Michael. However, there was one other person who was always in and out of the house, her name was Wilona. Wilona was a friend of the family. Because she was a friend of the family, Wilona not only had access to everything that was in the house, she also had access to the dialogue of the house. It didn't matter what was going on in the family, when Wilona walked through the door they would fill her in on everything that was happening.

In John 10:9 Jesus says, *"I am the door: by Me if any man enter in, he shall be saved, and shall go in and out, and find pasture."* In other words, in the Father's house, as you go through Jesus Who is the door, not only do you have access to everything in the house, but you have access to the dialogue of the house. It's a great thing to be a friend of this family, because you can also be made aware of the family secrets.

For example:

If I get sick, I know the dialogue that *"…by His stripes I am healed."*

If I'm struggling in my finances, I know the dialogue that I can call on Him as *Jehovah Jireh, the Lord Who will provide.*

If I'm dealing with anxiety, I know the dialogue that I don't have to be anxious for nothing, and with prayer and supplication with thanksgiving, I can make my request known unto Him and *"…the peace of God which surpasses all understanding will comfort and guard your heart and mind through Christ Jesus."*

In other words, it pays to be a friend of the family and we need to do whatever we need to do to stay in the family. So don't be carried away with every wind of doctrine. Don't be enticed by the pleasures of this world that lead to death. Stay focused. Keep your mind focused on Him. Whatever challenges you are dealing with today, whatever circumstances you are dealing with today, the good news is you are a friend of the family, and as a friend of the family you have access to everything you need to keep moving forward. I'm so grateful for my family, but oh how it pays to be a friend of His family!

A FRIEND OF THE FAMILY

Today's Prayer: Father, thank you for allowing me to be a part of Your family. Thank you that I am privy to the family secrets, where there is an answer in Your house to every problem I may be facing in my house. I'm grateful for my family, but what a blessing it is to be a friend of Your family. In Jesus' name, Amen!

DAY 17

"As the Father loved Me, I also have loved you; abide in My love. If you keep My commandments, you will abide in My love, just as I have kept My Father's commandments and abide in His love." (John 15:9–10)

SAFE IN HIS ARMS

On Day 1, I talked about how "Love Wins" as it becomes our weapon of choice. Love should be the response to everything negative that comes our way. Today, I want to talk about how love is a safe place of habitation that Jesus is calling us to abide in. The reason why the world is in the state it's in is because it doesn't know the love of Christ. The reason you may have grown up in a home where there was chaos, drama, and abuse is because the leader of the home didn't know the love of Christ.

Outside of His love, there is danger, but in abiding in His love, there is safety. This is why no matter what place you find yourself in physically, mentally, and emotionally, you should not only run to His love but stay there.

How do we abide in the safety of His love? Jesus says in John 15:10, *"If you keep My commandments, you will abide in My love, just as I have kept My Father's commandments and abide in His love."*

The word "if" is conditional, meaning we have a responsibility. If I keep His commandments, then I get to abide in His love. This means that knowledge of the Word of God enables me to counter every deceptive thing that comes against me, keeping me within the protective shield of His love. If you're going to be safe in His arms, then you must abide in the safety of His love, and to abide in the safety of His love means we must be obedient to the Word.

> *Today's Prayer: Father, I thank you that while I am living in a dangerous and fallen world, Your love is a place of safety where I can abide. I understand that outside of Your love is danger but keeping Your commandments keeps me within the safe confines of Your love. In Jesus' name, Amen!*

_____

_____

_____

_____

_____

_____

_____

DAY 18

"These things I have spoken to you, that My joy may remain in you, and that *your joy may be full."* (John 15:11)

FULL OF JOY

I remember running out of gas on the expressway. Thankfully, someone saw that I was stuck, volunteered to go to the nearest gas station, filled the red gas container with fuel, came back, and put the fuel in my tank so that I could keep going.

Referring back to yesterday, talking about the importance of obedience and how it allows us to abide in His love, Jesus is sharing these things because He knows the different things that life will throw at us can cause us to get stuck, so we're going to need the fuel of His joy to keep going. He says it needs to remain in you, which means that like I ran out of gas, you can run out of joy, and because there are others who need you, you cannot afford to run out of joy.

The Greek word for joy is *chara*. It means cheerfulness, calm, delight, gladness...

FULL OF JOY

So your obedience to His Word allows you to abide in His love, which enables His joy to remain in you, your joy being full so when you run up against an emergency, you can still be cheerful. When you run up against insurmountable problems, you can still remain calm. You may be in a situation where you don't know how it's going to turn out, but you can still remain glad and delight yourself in Him. Resolve today that nothing or nobody will deplete you of your joy. As you travel through the ups and downs of this life, you will remain "Full of Joy."

Today's Prayer: Father, I thank you for the instructions that my obedience to keep Your Word allows Your joy to remain in me, and that my joy will be full. Today, I commit to being diligent in allowing nothing or no one to steal my joy. I declare that through it all, the joy of the Lord is my strength. In Jesus' name, Amen!

DAY 19

"This is My commandment, that you love one another as I have loved you." (John 15:12)

SAFE IN MY ARMS

Day 17, which was "Safe in His Arms" spoke to how keeping His commandments enables us to abide in His love, which keeps us safe from everything deceptive in this world that is contrary to His love. However, His command to us to love one another as He has loved us keeps everyone who comes in contact with us safe in our arms. What's love got to do with it? Everything! As a believer in the Lord Jesus Christ, you should be a safe place. After someone has left your presence, they should be better off than they were when they came into it. Woe unto us, as ambassadors of Jesus Christ, if anyone should leave us worse off than they were when they came.

This also means that since Jesus was willing to lay down His life to show His love, so should we be willing to lay down our lives to show our love. This doesn't necessarily mean physically, but we should be willing to sacrifice for the well-being of others, which will prove that we are a friend of Christ, putting His love on display and being a safe place for others. Yes, walking in this love thing is a pretty big deal, considering we live in a world where there is so much hate and evil. Somebody needs to be the example. Why not you? Every person that comes in contact with you must feel that you're a safe place for them. There should be a willingness to repent for everyone we've ever done wrong, while going forward striving to do right by everyone we know and meet so that our testimony will be they were "Safe in My Arms."

Today's Prayer: Father, today I realize I have a tremendous responsibility as it pertains to everyone that comes in contact with me. Father, please forgive me for anyone and everyone I've ever mistreated. I want to represent You when it comes to my motives and actions toward others. I accept the assignment that You've given me to be a safe place for them. In Jesus' name, Amen!

_____

_____

_____

_____

_____

_____

_____

_____

DAY 20

"For if we believe that Jesus died and rose again, even so God will bring with Him those who sleep in Jesus. For this we say to you by the word of the Lord, that we who are alive and remain until the coming of the Lord will by no means precede those who are asleep. For the Lord Himself will descend from heaven with a shout, with the voice of an archangel, and with the trumpet of God. And the dead in Christ will rise first. Then we who are alive and remain shall be caught up together with them in the clouds to meet the Lord in the air. And thus we shall always be with the Lord." (1 Thessalonians 4:14–17)

FLOATING ON CLOUD NINE

With so much going on in this world today, it's always a blessing when good things happen. Whether it's getting a raise on your job, a new opportunity presented to you, or your child making the honor roll. It could be your child graduating, finally paying off a debt, or even meeting a new boo. It could be purchasing a new home, getting a new car, or finally getting free from a difficult situation. There are times in life where it seems like everything is coming together, things are lining up, and you're in a good place, so much so that you may say, "I'm floating on Cloud Nine."

However, there is a day coming where everyone who puts their faith and trust in Jesus Christ as the Son of God, Who alone is able to forgive sins, will one day be literally, "floating on Cloud Nine." He is going to descend from heaven with a shout. Those who have already passed will rise first, then those of us who are alive will be caught up together in the clouds to meet the Lord in the air, and so shall we ever be with the Lord. There is nothing that we will experience in this life that will compare to this "floating on Cloud Nine" experience. Be encouraged today that just as we look to escape difficulties in this life, there is a day coming where we will make the great escape out of this life, where pain and suffering will be no more. While I'm excited about my continued service to the Lord here, I'm looking forward to and know that nothing will compare to the day I'm "Floating on Cloud Nine."

FLOATING ON CLOUD NINE

Today's Prayer: Father, I'm so grateful for everything You've done for me while here in this life. You have provided a means for salvation in Jesus Christ, Your Son. You have kept me through every storm, and You have blessed me in so many ways. Yet still, I know the best is surely yet to come. Help me to remember the beauty of the big picture when I'm faced with the ugly of the small pictures. That day, I'll get to "float on Cloud Nine." In Jesus' name, Amen!

DAY 21

"Coming to Him as to a living stone, rejected indeed by men, but chosen by God and precious." (1 Peter 2:4)

HE CHOSE YOU!

If you live long enough, you will face rejection. It's an inevitable part of life. There are too many reasons to list why you may face rejection, but it is a very real reality. You may get rejected because of skin color. You may have been rejected by parents who didn't want the responsibility of raising you. You may have been rejected growing up by your peers because of how you looked, talked, or dressed. You may have experienced the deep pain of being rejected by a spouse who chose another. However, it's important to understand that the reason for being rejected is absolutely no indication of your true worth and value. Their rejection of you was actually protection for you. It was something you didn't need in your life anyway. Your true value is not found in being accepted by men, it's found in being accepted by God. He already chose you before the foundation of the world.

Our verse today speaks to how Jesus was rejected by men but chosen by God, and precious. If Jesus, Who is perfect, was rejected, that means we are in pretty good company. Their thoughts of Jesus did not change God's place for Him to be sitting at His right hand with all power. Their thoughts of you have not changed God's plan for you to be sitting in a place of love, joy, peace, and contentment because you realize you've already been chosen by the Creator before ever being rejected by His creations. Their response to who you are should hold absolutely no weight at all when you know that you've been chosen by God. Whether you are reading this before you start your day or before you go to bed, you can leave the house or go to sleep knowing that "He Chose You."

> *Today's Prayer: Father, I thank you that You love me with an everlasting love and You have chosen me. I'm grateful that my experience at the hands of them doesn't change who I am in You. I am chosen and beloved by my Father in heaven, and I will rest in this truth for the rest of my life. In Jesus' name, Amen!*

_____

_____

_____

_____

_____

_____

_____

DAY 22

"This is the message which we have heard from Him and declare to you, that God is light and in Him is no darkness at all. If we say that we have fellowship with Him, and walk in darkness, we lie and do not practice the truth. But if we walk in the light as He is in the light, we have fellowship with one another, and the blood of Jesus Christ His Son cleanses us from all sin." (1 John 1:5–7)

LET'S GO TO PRACTICE

My favorite player in the NBA today is Steph Curry. There hasn't been anyone in the history of the NBA that can shoot the ball like he does. His shot is so good that you really have to begin guarding him once he crosses half-court. He has amazed fans with what he's been able to do on the court publicly. However, what we see publicly is because of the practice that he puts in privately. If he chooses, Steph Curry cannot only talk about how good of a shooter he is, but he can back it up practically because of the practice that he puts in.

It's so important to understand that it's not enough to just talk about God. We must take it a step further and practice the truth that is laid out for us in His Word. So that, like Steph, when we are seen publicly, you can tell that we practice His truth privately. Professions of God without obedience to God are empty words. Jesus said in Matthew 15:8, *"These people draw near to Me with their mouth, And honor Me with their lips, But their heart is far from Me."*

Today we have an opportunity to no longer be "all talk" for God. Because we still have breath in our bodies, today we can "go to practice." We can walk in the light as He is in the light. We have the opportunity to no longer walk based on how we feel, but walk based on what His Word says. This means if it's OK in the Word then it's OK with me. This also means that if it's not OK in the Word then it's not OK with me. What do you say? "Let's Go To Practice."

LET'S GO TO PRACTICE

Today's Prayer: Father, I love You. I thank you for the opportunity to show my love for You not in word only but with my actions and my behavior. Father, please forgive me for all of the times I've misrepresented You knowingly and unknowingly. Today I'm commiting to daily "go to practice." I want to practice Your truth. In Jesus' name, Amen!

_____

_____

_____

_____

_____

_____

_____

DAY 23

"And when we all had fallen to the ground, I heard a voice speaking to me and saying in the Hebrew language, 'Saul, Saul, why are you persecuting Me? It is hard for you to kick against the goads.' So I said, 'Who are You, Lord?' And He said, 'I am Jesus, whom you are persecuting. But rise and stand on your feet; for I have appeared to you for this purpose, to make you a minister and a witness both of the things which you have seen and of the things which I will yet reveal to you.'" (Acts 26:14–16)

CAN I GET A WITNESS?

In the introduction of this book, I mentioned having a visitation one night. Shortly after repenting of my sins, confessing Jesus as my Savior and Lord, I was sleeping when my room became very bright. I looked up, and I believe it was a vision of Christ standing over me. He was so radiant and bright that I couldn't look at Him directly. I had to place my hand over my eyes as if I was trying to look at the *sun*, but clearly this was the *Son*. For years, I never understood why He appeared to me that night until one day reading our passage for today where *"...for I have appeared to you for this purpose, to make you a minister and a witness both of the things which you have seen, and the things which I will reveal to you."* (Acts 26:16*)* just leaped off the page at me.

The reason He appeared to Paul in this passage, and to me in 1999, is the same reason He has revealed Himself to you in one way or another, and that is so that you can be a witness to the things you have seen Him do, and to reveal what He has yet to reveal. Today, the Lord is asking you, "Can I Get a Witness? Can you vouch for me and tell others about the things you've seen Me do in your life? Can I Get a Witness?"

Tell someone how He has healed your body. Tell someone how He has provided for you and brought you increase. Tell someone how He has given you peace and joy in the midst of the most unfavorable circumstances. The goal is always to draw others to Him, and He has given all of us such a responsibility by asking us to be witnesses for Him.

CAN I GET A WITNESS?

Today's Prayer: Father, today I thank you for the many ways You have revealed Yourself to me. I thank You for Who You are, and all that You've done for me. Thank you for the privilege to be a witness for You on the earth, sharing Your goodness with others. In Jesus' name, Amen!

DAY 24

"Now when they had departed, behold, an angel of the Lord appeared to Joseph in a dream, saying, 'Arise, take the young Child and His mother, flee to Egypt, and stay there until I bring you word; for Herod will seek the young Child to destroy Him.' When he arose, he took the young Child and His mother by night and departed for Egypt." (Matthew 2:13–14)

PROTECT THE GIFT

The game of football is a game of transition. As you are transitioning down the field, en route to the goal line, it is imperative to protect the football that is in your hands. The worst thing that can happen is to have transitioned all the way down the field to the goal line and the enemy not only strips what you're carrying but recovers what you're carrying. So now instead of a touchdown, there is a let down because the enemy was able to take what was in your hands.

Just like God placed the gift of Jesus in the hands of Joseph to protect because the world would need Him, so has He placed a gift or gifts in your hands that the world needs, and just like

Joseph, your responsibility is to protect that gift. You cannot afford to fumble the gift that God has given you. What kept Jesus safe was Joseph's willingness to go exactly where God told Him to go and to stay there until God told Him to move.

The world needs the gift that you're carrying, and to ensure its safety it's best to not move outside of the will of God. When God says move, then you move. When God says stay, then you stay. If we choose not to use the GPS that He has provided for our lives, then those who are supposed to be on the receiving end of our gifts never will be. You were placed in this world to use your gift or gifts to bring Him glory and to bless others. Like Joseph, stay in step with God to ensure that you "Protect the Gift."

Today's Prayer: Father, thank you for entrusting me with a gift. I want to utilize that gift so that You are glorified. Help me to be sensitive to Your leading so that where You go, I'll follow. I don't want to waste Your gift, I want to protect it. In Jesus' name, Amen!

DAY 25

"And Pharaoh was angry with his two officers, the chief butler and the chief baker. So he put them in custody in the house of the captain of the guard, in the prison, the place where Joseph was confined. And the captain of the guard charged Joseph with them, and he served them; so they were in custody for a while." (Genesis 40:2–4)

SERVING IS THE KEY

Have you ever been falsely accused? Have you ever found yourself in a predicament that wasn't fair? Have you ever asked God, "Why am I in this place?" Joseph was on the receiving end of such an experience, serving time for a crime that he did not commit. Not only that, but they had the nerve to give Joseph the responsibility to serve people while he was in a place where he saw no way out.

Whenever we're in a difficult place where it seems like we're confined, it's easy to have the mindset that "I'm just going to do me." It's easy to say, "I don't have time to worry about others." However, Joseph's willingness to help others, while I'm sure he felt he needed help also, was the key that was about to unlock a great season of blessing for him.

Because he was willing to serve, Joseph was about to go from wearing prison clothes to wearing royal clothes. One of the people he served while in prison, the butler, got out of prison and had the ear of the very person who was about to change Joseph's life. Be very careful who you dismiss because life is not fair for you at the moment. Be very careful who you disregard because you've decided at this time it's all about you. The very person you help while in a confined place could be the one who knows the one who can bring you out. Serving is the key, because Pharoah unlocked Joseph's God-ordained future which came with promotion, wealth, and influence. I understand that you may be in a difficult place right now. However, continuing to serve others is the key that will ultimately unlock what God has for you.

SERVING IS THE KEY

Today's Prayer: Father, I'm going to be honest. I don't like this place that I'm in. Please help me to not only see my needs but also the needs of others. I understand that You've called me to be selfless, so here I am today, Your humble servant, willing to help and serve others because I understand that serving is the key. In Jesus' name, Amen!

_____
_____
_____
_____
_____
_____
_____
_____

DAY 26

"And supper being ended, the devil having already put it into the heart of Judas Iscariot, Simon's son, to betray Him, Jesus, knowing that the Father had given all things into His hands, and that He had come from God and was going to God." (John 13:2–3)

HE'S PROMISED

We're coming to the end of this thirty-day devotional. We've talked about how life is full of pain, problems, disappointments, setbacks, and obstacles. We've also talked about how abiding in His love helps us. We've talked about how keeping our joy full helps us. We've also looked into a glorious future for all believers, where we will leave this fallen world and everything that comes with it behind while being able to "float on Cloud Nine." You could say that these all fall under the umbrella of "His promises." If we were to condense what can keep you when you can't keep yourself, it would be knowing the promises of God. When you know what He's promised, you can handle any problem.

In our text today, Jesus is about to go through the pain of being betrayed by someone he walked closely with for three and a half years. He's also about to go through the physical pain of a crucifixion on the cross. I believe what enabled Him to make it through these challenges was what it says He knew in John 13:3, *"Jesus, knowing that the Father had given all things into His hands, and that He had come from God and was going to God."*

He knew what the Father promised, and He knew where and to Whom He was going. Like Jesus was hanging on that cross, you may feel like you're hanging on by a thread. It is knowing what "He's promised" you that will get you through and to everything that He has for you. If we have every intention to keep our promises to our natural children, then how much more does our Father in heaven intend to keep His promises to us. The best response when you don't like what you see or hear is knowing what "He's promised." Rest on His promises today that are found in His Word.

HE'S PROMISED

Today's Prayer: Father, I know that the devil is a liar, and Your Son Jesus is the Truth. When I'm facing uncertainty in my life, help me to shun the lie while gravitating toward the truth. I know the truth is found in Your promises, and so I'll rest on them. In Jesus' name, Amen!

DAY 27

"But whoever has this world's goods, and sees his brother in need, and shuts up his heart from him, how does the love of God abide in him? My little children, let us not love in word or in tongue, but in deed and in truth." (1 John 3:17–18)

A HELPING HAND

All you have to do is turn on the TV or drive ten miles, and you'll quickly see how much the world is in need. There are gaps all over the world that need to be filled. There are holes all over the world that need to be plugged, and God has placed you here for such a time as this. As believers, we have the responsibility to see a need and then see where we can fill in the gap. In other words, we need to have open hearts with open hands, willing to not only see a problem but also prepared to do something about it.

A HELPING HAND

This is another wonderful way and opportunity for us to be a witness for Him. This is another amazing chance to put the love of God on display. After we've heard about it, let's spring into action and do something about it. Jesus said, *"It is better to give than to receive."* What a privilege we have to be givers for the purposes of meeting a need, showing the love of God and where He is glorified as a result. Today, I would like to encourage you to shift from having tunnel vision to looking all around you and seeing who can benefit from you being a blessing to them.

Every season is a great season to give. This isn't always monetarily. You can always give of your time and your talents as well. Again, this is what Joseph did while in prison, that we covered two days ago. Does your local church have a need? Does your job have a need? Does the homeless man or woman have a need? Does your neighbor have a need? If not us, then who? If not now, then when? Today is a great day to see how you can be "A Helping Hand."

A HELPING HAND

Today's Prayer: Father, please open my eyes to the needs around me. Please show me what I have that I can give to help others. Help me to identify at least one person today to whom I can give of my time, talent, or treasure, glorifying You. I desire to give a helping hand. In Jesus' name, Amen!

_____

_____

_____

_____

_____

_____

_____

DAY 28

"But none of these things move me; nor do I count my life dear to myself, so that I may finish my race with joy, and the ministry which I received from the Lord Jesus, to testify to the gospel of the grace of God." (Acts 20:24)

I CAN'T BE MOVED

It is impossible to go through this life without having to deal with "these things." It's "these things" that will attempt to immobilize you, place fear in you, and hinder you to such a degree that you never become all that God intended you to become and you never do all that God intended you to do. This is the devil's plan, that you are moved off the course that God has planned for you, having been overcome by "these things." But I want you to declare out loud now, "I Can't Be Moved."

I love our passage for today, because if there is anybody that's had to deal with "these things," it's the Apostle Paul.

One example is the fact that he was stoned in Iconium, dragged out of the city, and left for dead. That's enough to make you say, "I'm done preaching this gospel stuff." However, the Bible says he continued preaching in another city and then went back into the city where he was stoned to encourage the disciples there to continue in the faith. Paul's mindset was that against all odds, he had to finish what God gave him to do. Not only that, but he was going to finish it with joy. If the Apostle Paul couldn't be moved after almost being stoned to death, but continued in the face of danger because His life was not his own, how much more should we continue against all odds, determined to finish what God has started in us. He does actually desire to finish what He's started.

"Being confident of this very thing, that He who has begun a good work in you will complete it until the day of Jesus Christ." (Philippians 1:6)

I know you see "these things," but I also know that just like the Apostle Paul, you "Can't Be Moved."

I CAN'T BE MOVED

Today's Prayer: Father, please strengthen me to continue the race that You've given me. Please help me to leap every hurdle and to not succumb to them. I declare that "these things" aren't bigger than my God Who enables me to overcome all things. I'm resolved today that I can't be moved. In Jesus' name, Amen!

DAY 29

"I have been crucified with Christ; it is no longer I who live, but Christ lives in me; and the life which I now live in the flesh I live by faith in the Son of God, who loved me and gave Himself for me." (Galatians 2:20)

I'M DEAD

I have to admit that I get a kick out of hearing the slang or the phrases said by the younger generation today. There are so many of them. One of those phrases in response to something that is hilariously funny or anything that's outrageous is the phrase "I'm dead." If you're on social media, you'll see them put the skeleton face emoji indicating this response. However, while that may be a term said by young people today, it should be a term lived by believers today. In other words, I must become numb to what I want to do so that I can come alive to what Christ wants to do in me.

In our verse today, the Apostle Paul gives us a great reason why we should live an "I'm dead" kind of life. It's because Jesus loves us, and He gave Himself for us. So if He was willing to give Himself for me, then the least I can do is to give myself to

I'M DEAD

Him. How do I give myself to Him? By not doing what I want to do, but doing what He wants to do. By not saying what I want to say, but saying what He wants to say. By not responding how I want to respond, but responding how He would want me to respond. There is a song by William McDowell that says, "My life is not my own, to You I belong, I give myself, I give myself to You." Today, what a privilege it is to have another opportunity to surrender to His will and His way. It's not until "I'm Dead", that I can really say that "I'm alive."

> *Today's Prayer: Father, thank you for Your death on the cross for me. Thank you for loving me not in words only but by proving it with action by giving Yourself for me. Father, I surrender my plans for Your plans. I surrender my words for Your words. I want to live such a crucified life so that when I'm asked, "How is it that you're so alive?" I can say, "It's because I'm dead". In Jesus' name, Amen!*

DAY 30

"Jesus answered and said to him, 'What I am doing you do not understand now, but you will know after this.'" (John 13:7)

YOUR NEXT SEASON WILL MAKE SENSE

If you've ever binge-watched anything on Netflix, then you know that in between the episode that you're watching now and the episode you're about to watch next, there are words at the bottom right of the TV that say, "Next Episode," and there is a bar loading that indicates that what you're currently watching is coming to an end, and what you're about to watch next is about to begin.

On the last day of this devotional, I would like to speak prophetically about your life by saying what you're currently watching now in your life is coming to an end, and what you're about to watch next in your life is about to begin. In other words, be encouraged because your "next episode" is loading. What's about to come on in your life is about to make sense. It's all going to come together. You will be able to exhale. You will be healed. You will see the provision. You will have the help that you need, and so on.

The disciples didn't understand why Jesus was washing their feet. It didn't make sense to them. *Jesus told them, "What I am doing you do not understand now, but you will know after this."*

You're getting ready to enter into a season in your life where it's all going to make sense. So the last thing you want to do is to give up now. The last thing you want to do is to cave in now. If you can obey God now, when it doesn't make sense, what's about to come next in your life will all be worth it. "Your Next Season Will Make Sense."

> *Today's Prayer: Father, I admit there has been a lot going on that I don't understand. This process has been long, and it has me weary. Father, please strengthen me as I'm coming to the end of this current episode in my life, and thank you for bringing clarity as the next episode begins. In Jesus' name, Amen!*

CONCLUSION

Thank you for taking this thirty-day journey with me. My sincere prayer is that you have been encouraged, inspired, enlightened, and even challenged. Since it's been about thirty days since you read Day 1, please feel free to take the journey again for another month, and as often as you'd like. Reminders and refreshers are always good.

My sincerest prayer is that if you've never taken advantage of the free offer in the introduction, you would go there now and take advantage of the amazing offer that will absolutely change your life and propel you to heights you've never imagined. Thank you again for indulging in *Let Me Encourage You: A 30-Day Devotional for Everyday Living*.

In Service to Him,

George Robinson

CONCLUSION

Made in the USA
Middletown, DE
28 December 2022